Seven Times Hotter

MY PERSONAL FIERY FURNANCE EXPERIENCE

Seven Times Hotter

My Personal Fiery Furnace Experience

Penned by
Xaviera L. Bell

Acknowledgement

There are so many things that I could say about the people that love me. To the women that allowed me to cry, that allowed me to vent, that allowed me to be weak without judgment. I appreciate you because without your active prayers and presence I am not sure if I would have made it out of the fire without evidence of the intense heat.

My pillars that held me on every side: Hazel Hill, Eran Woodyard, Ashley Bell Johnson, Gina Perryman, Jeanette Benjamin, Erica Ware, Monica Wilson, Belidania Oscar, Sheatell McGriff, Dionne Brunson, Lyvenie Sanon, Angel Johnson, Natalie Moore, Rolanda Dorange, and Alica Woodyard. For standing in the furnace with me, I'll forever love you!

To my daughter in my heart.. Even though your little brain can't understand the complexity of this ordeal, your heart felt my pain. I love you no matter how the story ends.

Lastly, to my ex.. The first man that I loved with my complete heart.. I thank you for the tragically beautiful love story.. You were my first lesson in love.. For that I am grateful.

To My Granny

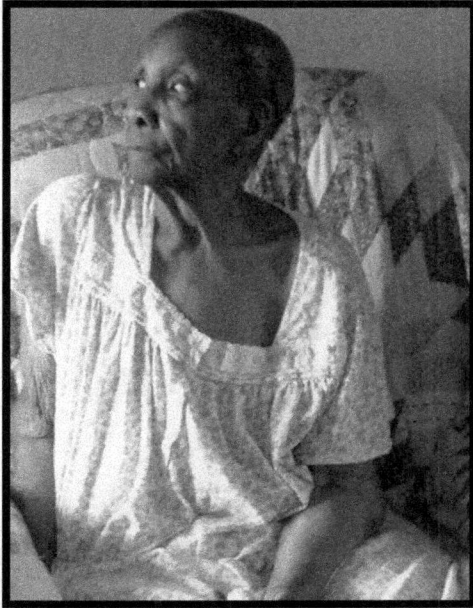

Marie Adams Thomas
October 30, 1924 – April 13, 2016

Thank you for being the most impeccable person that I know. Your grace and sweet heart has taught me that kindness is the key and usually the response to all situations. You have taught me so many lessons in life and daily I attempt to live a life that would make you proud. I thank God that in your older age that you never forgot us and if you did you were too kind to let us know that you didn't remember. I love you so much and I miss you.

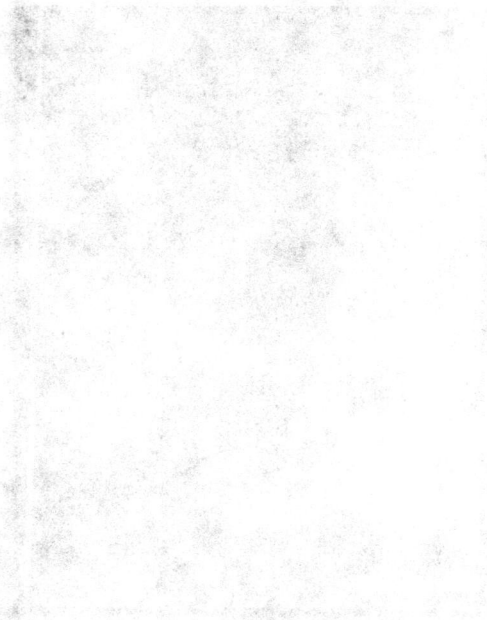

Table of Content

Introduction

The bible gives an account of three Hebrew boys being thrown into a fiery furnace. I know that we are all familiar with the story and that we have heard it more than once in a church service. However, what intrigued me with the story is that the king ordered that the heat in the furnace be increased seven times hotter than usual. When I read that the order was given to increase the temperature of the furnace I wondered if the king knew that there was something special about these individuals. I wondered did he recognize that they were so amazing that their particular situation and demise required additional heat. I also thought to myself, how inconsiderate of the king. How could he mandate that the furnace be increased so drastically that it killed the individuals that were ordered to deliver the three boys into the pit of fire?

This story is so close to my heart because as I stood in the middle of my furnace moment... God appeared. He surrounded me with people that guarded me, that lifted me, that covered me. He did not allow the individuals that delivered me into the fiery pit to on look and be satisfied with the death of me. In the belly of the pit, there was a transformation, there was a resurrection, and there was confirmation. But most of all in the belly of the furnace there was my life being refined in the temperatures that were supposed to destroy me. I survived, although the furnace was... Seven Times Hotter!

The Hunt: I Took the Bait

SEVEN TIMES HOTTER

There was nothing that stood out about him in particular. He was just intriguing. He was an extra spiritual church boy that wasn't on my radar because he was not my type at all. He was very handsome don't get me wrong but he was well under 6 feet tall and I loved the men that I dated to tower over me.

He was a familiar face in my office because he was closely acquainted with one of the secretaries. She considered him a "spiritual brother". He was present within the office a couple days out of the week. I can remember the first time that I noticed him. Although he was there often I never really paid attention to him. On this particular day he rang the loud silver bell that was located outside the office door. Since my office was closest to the door, the ding penetrated my being like a dagger. To say that I hated that bell was being courteous. As I approached the lobby desk my stare radiated my disgust. He appeared almost fearful. He stepped away from the bell and said, "I was just trying to let someone know I was here." I responded in a frustrated mother's tone, "We know you're here, you're always here. If you ring that bell again I will murder you. Now come in here and be quiet." He followed my direction and went straight to his sister's office with a smirk on his face.

In the office we all knew that he had fallen on

hard times, however, we didn't know the extent of what was happening in his life. We didn't know that his daily existence was a battle. But soon I would get an up close and personal escort through the hiccups of his life.

I remember the day that he approached me for a date. I was in his sister's office venting about the relationship that I decided to end. This wasn't unusual because I was always in her office talking about one thing or another. As I exited her office all while saying, "I'm done with him! I can't do this anymore!" He looked at me and said, "Are you free now?" In my head I thought he was being overly spiritual. I thought that he was asking have I released all the venom that I was spitting, have I been released from that ball and chain so that God could use me accordingly. I gazed at him in confusion and replied, "What?" He smiled and I noticed what appeared to be perfect white teeth, maybe his teeth were so white because his skin was so dark. He said, "Are you free? I mean are you free to go out?" I stood there in disbelief but I was amused by his nerve to approach me in that way. I said to him, "Come back in two weeks and I'll let you know."

As the two week mark approached we passed each other with smiles and acknowledgement of each other. It wasn't awkward or uncomfortable at all. I decided that the best thing to do is to ask his sister what he was all about and how she felt about me going out with him. When I asked her this question she told me that he was a good listener and that he is patient and he is fun. She thought that he would be a good person to give me a male perspective. I thought to myself, "a church boy, we will see where this thing goes."

On the fourteen day he approached me in my office. He asked, "So what's up? Are we going out or what?" I laughed hysterically because he came in with some petite girl that looked very annoyed that he left her in the common area and inquired with me about a date. I responded by saying, "I guess." He replied, "Okay, so have your people get with my people so that we can make this happen." From that point we exchanged numbers and later had a few phone conversations.

One August night I was headed to a late dinner with a friend and I received a call from him. I advised him that I was headed out to dinner and he asked if he could come along. I told him that it wouldn't be an issue, I gave him the location and surprisingly he showed up. He walked in so casual and cute, he had on a salmon colored Polo shirt, khaki shorts, and a pair of boat shoes. He came and took his seat beside me and we all had a great conversation. When the dinner ended he asked if he could come to my apartment so that we could talk. As he trailed me through the streets of Jacksonville, Florida I thought to myself, this guy is going to try me.

When we arrived to my residence we walked down the 13 stairs to my river front apartment. As key met lock I could hear his breathing increase. He was anxious. I turned the knob and I invited him in. I escorted him to the living room that was located in the back of the apartment. I walked to the blinds and opened them so that the reflection of the moon light could be seen as it danced across the river's surface. He approached me and he touched me, he secured my body close to his and I was so comfortable that I complied. His touch was familiar like he had been touching me for years. He told me that he had been celibate for a year and I didn't mind because I knew that his long time celibacy would end on this night and it did. I remember him sitting on the edge of my king sized bed with his forehead in his palm. He looked disappointed and he asked if we could just talk. I was aggravated, because talking about Jesus was not going to be okay at this point. What we just did... Jesus was nowhere in it.

What I noticed about that moment is that although he was convicted it didn't stop him from coming over. His conviction did not stop him from seeing me, it didn't stop him from calling me. He compromised his soul or was I selling mine at a cheaply discounted rate.

His visits became frequent and although this was not my usual encounter I didn't mind the welcomed intrusion. One particular night I sat straddling his lap and he rubbed his hand over the tattoo on my thigh and he looked up at me and said, "When I'm with you, I feel like I'm with a bad girl." I didn't think too long or hard about the statement. But as I think back to that moment I wonder if he was chasing an experience.

When I look at this encounter I see so many errors. I see so many opportunities to run, however, my curiosity got the best of me. I wanted what he appeared to have, a relationship with God, I just didn't know that he was in the same position as I was. I was lost. I was in a downward spiral of self-gratification because my flesh was loose.

I figured out that he was drawn to me not because I was pretty (don't get me wrong I know that I am) but he was drawn to me because he and I had like spirits. We were so sexually connected that there was no need for direction or instruction, we knew what each other desired because the familiar spirits within us had communed. Don't think for one second that you are attracted to people by chance. This is absolutely not the truth, there are spirits assigned to you that lure you to the wrong connections.

When God was dealing with me about the hunt he brought a scripture to my mind. The scripture says:

> **"Stay alert! Watch out for your great enemy, the devil. He prowls around like a roaring lion, looking for someone to devour. Stand firm against him, and be strong in your faith. Remember that your family of believers all over the world is going through the same kind of suffering you are." (1 Peter 5:8-9, NLT)**

Now, am I saying that he was the devil, no I am not. But what I am saying is that I was not alert, instead of watching out for the enemy I entertained the enemy. Because I was living in a mess of an existence I looked to the hunter to provide me with stability and his footing was uncertain. We look to people that are doing a little better than we are. We find comfort in those people because they are flawed and we won't feel judged because they are in a mess.

I did not stand firm. I had both feet planted in sexual sin and it had become comfortable to me. Because he was battling a spirit of perversion I intrigued him and that drew him to me. We are on the hunt for imperfection because we don't want to be accountable for our imperfectness. We do not want the responsibility of walking upright in the Lord because leaning on a crutch takes the brunt of the weight.

I fell for the bait! The enemy knew that I was looking for a way out and he sent him along. Because he was a man of faith and he could speak in tongues and pray but he had a dark side of sin, it made me comfortable. I needed God but I wasn't looking for him in the church, I wasn't looking for him in the scriptures, I was looking for him in an imperfect shell of a being that had more issues than I did.

I fell hard. I was free falling while doing a somersault and I landed in a place that was unfamiliar. I was caged, I was in love.

SEVEN TIMES HOTTER

XAVIERA L. BELL

The Courtship: The Ups and Downs of the Romance

SEVEN TIMES HOTTER

I recall driving down Merrill Rd., we were headed out to spend some time together, which is what we usually did on Saturday. His words were so certain. I will never forget when he said, "I just want you to know that I am not going to see anyone else. And I wouldn't mind if you didn't see anyone else either." Now, my immediate reaction was to crash the car because this was a conversation that I was not ready to have. My response, "Okay. Well, I guess I won't see anyone else either." I was in shock because I thought that this was a faux relationship. I thought that we were pretending to be together, you know without the commitment. But I guess I was on the wrong page.

Things took off like a fire in a dry forest. One thing after another started to happen. He was kicked out of the all men's boarding house that he was staying in and he had no place to go. So of course, I invited him to live with me. I had two roommates and they were not opposed to it. He was the perfect guy, we cooked together, he washed the dishes, we had in-depth conversation about the word of God, all while sleeping on a defiled bed.

One particular night while sleeping I had a dream. The dream was about a sacrifice that was taking place in an open field that had a stream that ran in the middle. The dream was so intense that I woke up screaming. I laid there for a second to gather myself so that I could fall back asleep. While lying there, out of my peripheral I saw a lady walking from the on-suite passed the foot of my king sized bed and she stood at the window that looked out onto the lanai. She was lean and regal, she walked in confidence and arrogance. She walked as if she came to accomplish a goal and she intended on ensuring that she completed her mission. I watched in silence but surprisingly I was not terrified, I just wanted to know what she was doing there. I saw her pick up three white boxes that varied in size. She sat each one outside the window. When her task was complete she turned to walk back in the direction that she came. As she got to the middle of the bed she stopped and she looked at me and she whispered a word that was not in English. She then came to my side of the bed and stood beside me. She reached her hand over my body and attempted to touch him. I was shocked so I took my forearm and I hit her arm as hard as I could. When I made contact with her she disappeared. Immediately I began to attempt to wake him but nothing was working, not even the dogs that slept on the foot of the bed were waking up.

I shook him relentlessly, no response. I took my fist and I began to beat him repeatedly, finally he woke up. Out of his sleep he said, "What is your problem?" He got out of bed and went to the bathroom. When he returned he asked why I was

16

acting so crazy. I looked at him and the words that came out of my mouth scare me even now. I said, "The spirit of the Lord says that you have three witches assigned to you. I need to know what's going on!" His face was stunned. He said, "Wow." He began to tell me about a family member that dabbled in witchcraft that made an attempt to sacrifice him as a warlock. We talked for most of the night and when it was time to go back to sleep I was reluctant because I didn't know if she would return. He looked at me and assured me that all would be well. He said with compassion, "She's not coming back. Just hold on to me and sleep."

The next morning we continued our conversation and I decided to research the word that she whispered. At the time I didn't know how significant it was but now I realize that she whispered a spell over the beings in the room. After researching I found that the word was Egyptian and it meant to be put in a sleeping trance. This means that all human beings and animals that were under the sound of these words would be placed in a deep sleep and would not be able to be awakened until it was lifted. I always wondered why I did not fall asleep.

From that point it seemed that there was always something in the relationship. It was like a whirlwind. When we were good, we were really good and when we were not, we were not!

Five months into our relationship I met his family. To some this isn't a big deal but after noticing the strained communication between them I needed to meet them. If this man was going to be with me I had to meet the people that knew him best. Everyone was so kind and welcoming. I was so afraid because here I am a country black girl meeting a Haitian family, I didn't know the language and I didn't know the customs. All I knew is that I was there. During this meeting I also met his daughter, who had just turned 2. I fell hard. She was the sweetest baby and she took to me immediately. My heart was captivated and I didn't even know it.

I look at all the warning signs and for some reason I thought that I could change him. While at dinner one night during our visit his cousin asked, "So, why are you with him? I mean it seems that you have yourself together. You're established and smart. Why are you with him, because he's going to mess this up?" I chuckled. But in my heart I knew it was true. It was like God was giving me so many signs and I was ignoring them.

After concluding our visit with his family I returned to work. In order to catch up on the weekend workload I stayed later than usual. While sitting at my desk I was approached by his "spiritual sister," She came to me and said, "I know you are in love with my brother but he doesn't love you." It deflated me. It bruised me. I wondered why would a person say that to someone, was that what friendship looked like. The last portion of my employment was difficult. It became uncomfortable. There was tension and always something being said about our relationship by the "spiritual mother" and/or the "spiritual sister". The "spiritual mother" went as far as to contact the pastor of a church that I was attending to ask him questions, talking negatively about me, and defaming my character. Every level of disrespect was shown at this time. I was standing in a place of darkness and it was all at the hands of women that loved God, that heard God, that prayed, that spoke in tongues. But where was God in this situation?

I started noticing a great deal of inconsistencies. He would go for long walks outside with the cell phone. I got smart. Not only did I start checking the numbers I had a tracking device on the phone. Which came in handy the day I told him to leave.

I noticed that there were a great deal of text messages from women and one in particular from his ex. I was nosey and I read it. The saying is true. When you look for something you will definitely find it. I was outraged. I was floored. I was so bothered that I woke him up and addressed the issue at hand. It was so heated that the end result was him packing his things and me dropping him off at the train station.

That train station was so pivotal in our relationship. I recall dropping him off one weekend after he spent days sleeping in the closet fasting and praying. He slept on the floor of the closet for days, saying that God wants him to return to down south Florida and cut all ties with his previous girlfriend that he was off and on with for the last 13 years. That God said he must release her and her children so that he could move forward with me. Lets just say as the story unfolded the only thing that was released was himself in her.

Even as God reminds me of these experiences I am saddened. I remember this so vividly. I recollect how it felt to lay in the doctor's office on a cold bed and the doctor says, "It appears that this was a chemical pregnancy and it didn't last. You're not pregnant at this point." I was alone, I was broken. As the tears released from my eyes and saturated the sides of my hair I digressed in that moment from the woman that God made me to simply average. I became typical in my thoughts and expectations in that moment because all I wanted was him to be there with me. He wasn't. According to the GPS on the phone he was down south sitting in the den of the house with a faux family pretending that things were perfect. I was experiencing the most detrimental time of my life and he was entertaining a soul tie that he conveniently kept open just to ensure he had a fall back plan.

The tears that I shed in the parking lot of that station. The hugs and the kisses that were exchanged, right in that parking lot. When I told him that he had to leave the intention was for him to be gone for good. My intention was to leave him in that parking lot and never look back. However, it didn't work out that way.

July 4th weekend of 2011 my parents came to town. We had plans to just enjoy ourselves and invite a few people over. He was missing so my mother inquired of his whereabouts. I told her that he had arrived in town but he was staying at the local shelter. Soon after her interrogation he called me, my mother overheard the conversation and the fact that he had not eaten in days. That's all she had to hear, she looked at me with pity and directed me, "Go get that boy. Nobody should have to live like that." I did as she directed. When he walked through the door, looking in on the situation, one could've easily thought that my mother was his mother. He fell into her arms and he began to apologize. She fed him until he was physically sick. When my parents left my father looked him in the eyes while giving him a firm hand shake and advised him, "Make good decisions." He replied with, "Yes sir."

I wish that I could say that things got better. That we became this power couple, we didn't. I made a decision to leave Jacksonville in September 2011 and return to Alabama. This was short lived and I have always wondered if I returned because I wanted to save him. I received nightly calls from random places that he was staying in the city. He frequented motels, all night facilities like Laundromats. I prayed often for his safety and I worried about him on a consistent basis. My time in Alabama was cut down to 64 days and I was back in Jacksonville. I had a friend that allowed me to stay with her and eventually he followed because he was not able to stay at the shelter because his work schedule wouldn't allow him to make the line in time to get in. We stayed for a few months and then she advised that he would have to vacate because of the apartment guidelines. My brain was in overdrive. What was I going to do? How could I be comfortable sleeping at night knowing that he was in a shelter or that he was sleeping outside somewhere? I was trying to figure out what I could do to get us a place to stay. I saved money and within 45 days I found an apartment in the St. Nicholas area. We were back together and I was happy, I was satisfied, I was content.

I was satisfied during this time being the average common law wife. Cooking dinners that he loved, having sex when he wanted to, and making sure that he was at work on time. Nothing like the life that I remembered. I had settled. Why? For what? His outside conversations continued, his walking around the neighborhood praying, his random confessions of love persisted. But that was short lived when he came into my bedroom and kissed me in the early hours of the morning saying that he would return in a couple of days. A few weeks before his departure I decided that we need to stop sleeping in the same bed so that we could wean ourselves from being sexual. I wanted so much to please God that I thought that two bedroom doors and a hallway would stop us. It didn't. We just made nightly visits to each other's rooms, indulged in sin, and came back to our rooms to marinate in it. On the afternoon of his departure I received an email from his ex (who obviously wasn't his ex) telling me that he was in route and they were to be married the next week. I went off like a bomb. I explained to her that there was no way that he would marry her because he had to be at work Monday and the courthouse was closed until Tuesday because of the holiday. What I knew was that he wasn't going to stay that long, because he grew bored with her easily. I also informed her that his Kenneth Cole slacks, shirt, and tie were still in the closet, so he'll be back.

When he returned I could hear his key hit the door knob. I didn't shift in my bed. Just having him back home made me feel better but really I was the biggest loser. Several hours later I heard him leave for work in the wee hours of the morning. He walked nearly 12 miles to work that morning all because he was caught. How funny it is that being in a self-created mess will inconvenience your life, then you have the nerve to be mad at the world and not holding your own self responsible. Was I angry for a while, yes, but we made up in the way that we knew how. After that everything was great.

December 2012 I lost my job and he had to step up to the plate as the bread winner. To my surprise he did. He grew so accustomed to me being home, pretending to be a stay at home wife, that he was nowhere near pleased when I took a job making $9 an hour at the hotel just to have an income. My advancement took off within the company and within 6 months I was the manager of the hotel. During this transition he advised me that it was time for him to relocate to Tampa so that he could start the ministry that he desired. I obliged and saw him off August of 2013. It broke my heart but I knew that if God had called him that I couldn't keep him from it. He visited on a consistent basis. He called daily and we courted in his physical absence.

One particular day he came to Jacksonville from Tampa and I told him that he needed to make a decision about our future. I told him in this moment, "You need to decide if we are getting married and if not you need to leave and never look back." He agreed that we should get married and I started to plan. I picked out a 3 carat black diamond solitaire that I named Sabrina. She was beautiful. He liked it as well. November came and I made a trip to Tampa as his fiancé to help him host a women's conference. December came and he came to Jacksonville for Christmas. Things were normal, things felt right but God was tugging on me to adopt a lifestyle of celibacy.

In January 2014, I made a surprise trip to Tampa. When I showed up he was so fearful, he said with concern, "I thought that you were coming to break up with me." I looked at him in certainty and assured, "I am. Depending on how you respond." He asked if we could go somewhere to talk privately. We went to a local eatery and had a conversation, then we went to a park that we frequented every time I came to Tampa. We sat on the bench holding hands and I poured my heart out to him. I remember looking at him saying, "I love you. I'm in love with you and I have been for all these years. I want to be your wife. I want you to be the father of my babies. I want you to be my partner in ministry. But we can't move forward if you won't make that commitment." He just stared at me. He hung his head and replied, "Zay, I'm a mess. My life is a mess. I wouldn't even want to marry me. If you could just give me 2 years, let me work some things out. I promise you, I'm going to marry you. Just give me that time to get some things worked out." I was crushed. I felt rejected. I felt defeated. I felt unloved. He made up for the blow to my heart that night by doing what he did best. I remembered looking at the ceiling and thinking that this would be the last time we would have sex and not be married.

I look back at all the signs and instability of it all and wonder why I didn't just leave. Was I in love or lust? Had I sacrificed my soul for temporary satisfaction? Had I lost my good sense? Why was I being so desperate and so silly when I knew that God had destined me for greater? Because I had a soul-tie that I wasn't strong enough too severe.

I was thinking about the relevance of soul-ties and how they are destroying the lives of women all over this world. Killing our friends, our sisters, the woman in the neighboring apartment that was once so vibrant and now she's hollow. These soul-ties are specifically why there are so many women being killed by their mates because they stayed a little too long. Soul-ties are the reason that your daughter or sister won't leave when you tell her that he is cheating and that he means her no good.

God led me to a few scriptures but these two scriptures stuck out to me:

> **"And don't you realize that if a man joins himself to a prostitute, he becomes one body with her? For the Scriptures say, "The two are united into one." (1 Corinthians 6:16, NLT)**

> **"Run from sexual sin! No other sin so clearly affects the body as this one does. For sexual immorality is a sin against your own body." (1 Corinthians 6:18, NLT)**

Some might wonder how a soul-tie is created. The answer to that is so simple, agreement. When we are sexual with someone we have to come in agreement with that person to lie down and give ourselves to them. Sex is not the only way to create a soul tie. A soul-tie can be created by a close relationship and also by making a vow to be there for one another forever. However, all of these actions have agreement at its root.

When we are sexual with other individuals we come into agreement with the spirit that inhabits them. There are times that we find ourselves doing things that we would not normally do or craving things that we would not normally crave. Our desires change because we have to feed the spirit that now lives within us. This is extremely dangerous because soul ties are created to bind you to an individual, if you are not married to this person then you have signed up to for bondage.

The Chastity Mandate: It's Under Lock & Key

SEVEN TIMES HOTTER

When I left Tampa I received a call from him. Telling me that he loved me but he just needed the time. I told that I couldn't wait on him for 2 additional years. I advised him that I would still see him but I would be open to dating other people if the opportunity presented itself. I told him that I had made a decision to take a vow of celibacy that I decided to get real with God so that he would get real with me. He told me that he was proud of me and that he respected my decision to take a stand for godly principles. His words were so shallow. I knew that whenever the opportunity presented itself he would at least try. I was absolutely right. Shortly after my return to Jacksonville he came for a visit. He stayed for several hours and wanted to take a nap together. I knew in that moment that I would have to be strong willed because he too was my Achilles heel. I laid in the king sized bed that we once shared with him. It felt like old times. We cuddled and then he told me in his breathless voice, "I need you. I need us. I need that connection that we have." My response, "I'm sorry but the only thing that I can offer you is a nap." He was floored because I said no, very politely. He was visibly uncomfortable because his body wanted what it wanted and I was in no position to accommodate his flesh while compromising mine. Needless to say, he left my apartment unsatisfied and that satisfied me. But honestly, I didn't know how many more no's I would be able to give him.

God is so strategic in everything. Because he knew my weakness he placed even more distance between us. I lost my job in Jacksonville at the end of February and relocated back to Alabama in March 2014. As the months progressed I grew stronger. I was confident in my celibacy and I was not compromising that for him. I was put to the test in May of that year when I visited the area to see two clients that I had. While there I saw him on his birthday. I'll never forget May 21st. We've been so many places for his birthday, Atlanta, Savannah, and so forth. But this trip was so strange. I was supposed to pick him up from work so that we could spend some time together but I was so caught up in worship in the car that I took 95 South to Palm Bay, which put me 2 hours behind. When I got there he had been waiting hours and I felt so badly. I had planned a picnic for his celebration so we went to the park where we ate sub sandwiches and he had a carrot cake. We sat at the picnic table across from each other and he looked different to me. I asked him what was wrong and his response was, "I'm not myself. I'm going through a lot. I'm just depressed." My heart broke for him. I asked, "Do you need a hug?" He responded, "Yes please." I told him to come take a seat beside me and I embraced him, gave him a kiss on the forehead, and I scratched his back, which was his most favorite thing. He asked me to walk down to the water with him, he grabbed my hand and we took the short stroll. He told me that he was supposed to be meeting some coworkers that wanted to celebrate his birthday at Y'bor City's Jazz House. I was devastated but I didn't show it. I dropped him off at his coworker's house and proceeded to drive to his sister's apartment. He called me on my way and he could tell that I was disappointed. As I made my way to the hotel I received another call from him. He said, "You sound like you're still driving. Where are you going?" In annoyance I responded, "I'm headed to the hotel." He continued the conversation asking me what hotel I was staying at so that he could come visit me. So that we could spend more time together. I snapped. All that I can remember from that conversation is saying, "Listen, I came here to celebrate on your day and you're going to a café with people that you see on a regular basis. You have to be kidding me. You haven't seen me in months.. months. I just didn't pop up, you knew that I was coming to town. You're where you wanna be. Be there, stop calling me." My rant didn't stop him from calling, he called me from the bathroom of the café telling me that he wanted to come see me. I ended the call and went to sleep.

The next day we had a meeting with my client who was a friend of his father's. I went to pick him up from work and we went to meet with the couple, who were active in ministry. On our way to the meeting he wanted to know if I would allow him to buy me the Mother's Day gift that he asked could he buy me previously. I looked at him with rage and responded, "Our child is dead." He said, "But you'll always be the mother of my child." When we pulled into the driveway we pretended that we weren't having a dispute, we went with business as usual. During the meeting my client looked at me and said that she loved us as a couple and that she knew that God was going to do great things with us. At the conclusion of the meeting we all joined hands and prayed. They prayed for our ministry and us as a couple. It seemed to be the longest drive, we had surface conversation and I dropped him off and I continued to my hotel. He called me and said that he wanted me to come back to get him so that he could come over and we could spend quality time at the hotel. I wished him a good night and ended the call.

When I made it home the next week I was floored. I wondered why sex changes people. Because it was very clear that there was a disconnect and it was directly associated with the fact that I was celibate. Our communication was sparse but he did tell me that he would rather not be around me so that he wouldn't disrespect me. He said that he wanted to be in a sexual relationship and that he wasn't ready to give that part of us up. He explained that when he sees me his thoughts are consumed with being with me in a sexual capacity and he would rather stay away.

I was baffled. Because he and I served the same God. We loved the same God. Why was I convicted and he wasn't? Why did he believe that we could ask for forgiveness and things would be okay?

I can clearly remember several conversations that we had that resulted in him asking me to consider reigniting our sexual relationship. He said in boldness, "I tell you what. I will sign a contract that says immediately after we have sex we can go to the courthouse and be married." I was so confused. My response to him was, "What type of fool do you think I am? If you want sex that bad we can ditch the contract and just got straight to the courthouse. Because ultimately we are going to do what's right."

The conversations that we had about the lacking sexual component of our relationship were innumerable. This was an area that he wanted me to compromise, he wanted me to bend, and he wanted me to break my vow to God. I was not in any position to do that because I wanted God more than I wanted him.

This is what happens when we are lacking relationship with God. As women we try to fill a God void with a man, then we are surprised to learn that he not equipped to love us as Christ has directed. During those conversations I recognized what happened, my priorities shifted and he had not caught up. He was still caught up on the mediocre existence that we had previously and he was satisfied with settling.

The bible is clear about the expectation of God. Sex before marriage is forbidden, however, we get so physically led that we compromise our spiritual existence. The scripture says:

> **Let there be no sexual immorality, impurity, or greed among you. Such sins have no place among God's people. (Ephesians 5:3, NLT)**

These instructions are clear but at some point we figured that it didn't work for us. There are women that have been in relationships for years and have not gotten married because they are providing marital benefits without the sanctity of marriage. You've put yourself on the clearance rack and you're disappointed because you're not getting the commitment. This is a situation that you have control of, if you want more then you should mandate more.

Now, you will get those church men that will convince you that God is a forgiving God and that you can ask for forgiveness at any time. Read the scripture below:

Dear friends, if we deliberately continue sinning after we have received knowledge of the truth, there is no longer any sacrifice that will cover these sins. (Hebrews 10:26, NLT)

Do not think for a moment that there is a loophole in the scriptures. There's no way that you can live in agreement with Christ and satisfy your worldly desires, IT'S NOT POSSIBLE! The bible is clear, once you have knowledge of the truth it's not as simple as you saying, "God please forgive me for the sex that I just had. I know it's wrong." It is imperative that we understand that we are hand delivering our souls to the devil because we want to be satisfied sexually. Moments of satisfaction is resulting in an eternity of damnation.

The countless tears and nights of being with someone and still feeling alone. The things that aren't adding up. The babies that you have to raise alone because their fathers are ghost or involved in some other relationship. The heartbreak of waiting year after year because someone spoke out of turn and told you that this man was your husband and he is not committing to you. The keys that you have to keep asking for because you freely gave it to the wrong person.

God has called women to be so much more than we are living up to. We have become distracted by men and our involvements with them. Aren't you tired yet?

XAVIERA L. BELL

The Greatest Deception

Original Poem Written by: Xaviera L. Bell

SEVEN TIMES HOTTER

THE GREAT DECEPTION

A single touch of the hand intrigued me. It wasn't the touch but the spark that was ignited within me. The conversations that made love to my mind made me fall, it was a whirlwind and my life was shaken up by the twister that you were and I was displaced like a victim that was left abandoned with nothing to run to. You closed a chapter in my life without my permission and you have not allowed me to write my ending because you've kept the book open because you were not equipped to totally walk away. You told me with your actions that spewed like venom on the pages that we created that I wasn't enough for you. The words that were formed by the love that we made were so temporary in this life's chapter that they vanished without a trace and I stand broken with pen in hand trying to remember what we had but it's been enveloped by the harshness of you.

How could 1+1=2 and still be wrong? How could me plus you equal us and still be wrong? How could the beat of my heart pause in my chest and the inhale of oxygen expand my breast at the very thought of you and still be wrong.

I believed you when you held me and the promises that were whispered in my ear that we would build a life and I would be your wife. I, waited for you to arrive at your fullest potential, I was thinking commercial and you were residential. You put us in a box and deprived us of growth because you knew that there was no future to us. You knew that you had no intention to build with me because you weren't skilled enough to see who I really was. I was more than just a body that kept you warm night after night. I was the tear that you released and the prayer that was laid at God's feet on behalf of us. I was your juice but you were too noosed by the concept that love would someday end, so you put me in the category of enemy instead of a lover and a friend.

How could 1+1=2 and still be wrong? How could me plus you equal us and still be wrong? How could the beat of my heart pause in my chest and the inhale of oxygen expand my breast at the very thought of you and still be wrong.

I sit in my thoughts and my feelings and question the validity of you. How could you deceive the very person that saved you from you? How could you decide that it was done without even consulting me? I was supposed to be the answers to your dreams and I never considered that you were a camouflaged nightmare. You know that thing that appeared to be greatness but was just a learned behavior because you had watched enough Lifetime to appear that you had substance, all the while I had settled for a nothing. The emptiness of your apology left me numb and then I realized that this is who you are, empty. I never considered that your emptiness sought me out because I was full of the light that you so desired. And even in your departure you fear returning to an existence without me. Your, I miss you's and I made a mistake text means nothing because you are married to your situation and there's no getting better for you. You can't be better because you are not true to you. You have returned to the hole that you once dug and the hand that I extended is now retracted because I will not save you. I realize that the hole that you created is big enough for two and I refuse to keep you company in the hole you dug for you. The truth is I'm better than you.

But how could 1+1=2 and still be wrong? How could me plus you equal us and still be wrong? How could the beat of my heart pause in my chest and the inhale of oxygen expand my breast at the very thought of you and still be wrong. It's wrong because of the deceit of it all. You created a façade that you were not able to keep up. Being true was too much work for you. Accountability and compromise was far down your list and while I was enhancing you, you were digging a ditch for me. Secretly. Because a life with you for me was doable and all this time you were planning my emotional funeral. I shudder at the thought that I was almost lost in a situation that was destined for failure and I sit here and I can't pull myself together. Because I'm mad at you and what's ridiculous is that I have to explain why because you have no clue. That's more than enough reason to bounce and be done with you! Forever.

However, through it all I must give thanks that he made me strong enough to recover and save the love that he created in me for another. That the damage that you caused was all for my good and even thought I shouldn't I know that I could, forgive you. Because you're way more damaged than what you thought you did to me. You're flawed beyond repair and the next victim thinks they are getting a bargain but there's no value to you. Like putting money in a pocket and expect a return. There's no getting better and no matter how long they stay on their knees there's no better for you. Even if they weather the storm there is nothing that they could do because you're in control of you, and being common and deceitful is what's desirable for you. I thank God for my experience and this new direction but most of all I thank him for uncovering.. the greatest deception.

When You Know Better, You Do Better.. Right?

SEVEN TIMES HOTTER

There were so many inconsistencies that I should not have ignored. I should have ran before I was sucked in too deep. I stayed because I thought that the man that I had devoted years to was the man that was going to be my husband. I wondered why not only was I blinded by love but everyone that knew us was so sure that we were going to be a dynamic couple in ministry that they were blinded as well. People were routing for us and then there were also people praying against us.

There is nothing that you can do with a man that has another woman of influence in his ear. When I look back I recognize that I was fighting a losing battle for years. That no matter how much I tried to fix him or make his life comfortable, I may have temporarily had his heart, but I did not have influence over him. The dangers of that.

When a man shows you who he is believe it. When he exposes things during pillow talk, they're true. One day he said to me, "My spiritual mother said that I can't marry you because you'll ruin my ministry like my mother did my father's." I became immediately offended. My response to him, "I don't think that it's wise to take advice about marriage from someone that has never had a husband." He told me a lot in that moment. I was too busy trying to fight against it to just receive it and move forward, without him.

It is dangerous to skip courtship and merge right into the relationship lane. If I had spent time learning him, if I had not swan dived right into the bed with this "man of God" then I would have avoided the curse of the Church Playa. You know him. The single man in the church that can pray and always has a word from the Lord. So sanctified and sinful. The man that gives the greatest advise and he's a great listener. The man that rubs your feet and brings you apple juice with no expectation of anything in return, that's him. The fill in boyfriend. The one that you accidentally have sex with and then you two pray about it, however, that doesn't stop you from continuing.

I was bamboozled by the appearance of what I thought was holy. Because I had not tapped into discernment I was going off of my own logic, my own perception. On the evening that his spiritual sister told me that he didn't love me, she went on to tell me that he had not terminated his relationship with his ex-girlfriend. That his family was just happy to have someone else take up the brunt of the responsibility for caring for him. It seemed like he was in tuned with what was happening because he called several times and he even showed up to my office, all while she was sitting in my office serving me several blows to my heart. On the ride home I told him what happened, immediately he was infuriated. "Zay, I love you. I'm sorry that you have to go through this and I know being with me isn't easy. Dealing with them and all the other stuff. But I love you I do. I hoped you could see that. I love you."

That was the most silent ride home. I looked out of the window and I wondered how I got into this situation.

In May 2011, I was given the opportunity to go to a training with my job for 10 days in Tallahassee. The last week that I was there I was responsible for writing and presenting my own curriculum. While I was in Tallahassee I noticed that he didn't logoff of a social media site when he used the laptop. I being very inquisitive looked through his mail and confirmed what I knew was true, he was in fact interacting with other women. Being Zay, I decided to change his relationship status to in a relationship with, Xaviera 'Zay' Bell. Let's just say that this created a mess. When I returned to Jacksonville he had roses on the dresser and he gave every ounce of the attention that I needed. He helped me with my presentation and was chauffeuring me around town to find a copy center. While in route he received a telephone call, I could hear the panic from the individual that had contacted him and I knew immediately what it was in reference to. When arrived home he told me that he needed to talk to me about something. My response, "So your ex saw that I changed you relationship status.. She's upset.. Now what?" He was shocked. He started to tell me things about his past and specifically his past with her. I looked at him and asked, "Did you sleep with her when you went there to cut ties? That's all I want to know." He looked at me and responded, "Zay." I broke like a dam, the tears flowed and I couldn't even make out what I was saying to him. He held me and said, "I'm so sorry." Between whimpers I said, "But it's me. I would never hurt you. I've never done anything to hurt you. Why? Why would you do this? Why damage us?" He had no answers. All he could do was delete his account in good faith.

As a woman you have an expectation of a man. You have a list of deal breakers and principles that he must possess. But what happens when he breaks all the deal breakers and possess only half of the principles and you're still in love. What do you do when you've stayed through all the infidelity and the lies? I was in a position where I knew better but I wasn't exemplifying that knowledge of "the know". I was standing at the bottom of a pit praying that the love of my life would wake up one day and miraculously become the man that he thought he was.. he didn't.

XAVIERA L. BELL

Church Player

A Personal Poem Written by Xaviera L. Bell

SEVEN TIMES HOTTER

CHURCH PLAYER

I've been hoodwinked, bamboozled, I've simply been made a fool. I wrapped myself in the intentions and perceptions of you that the very application of my enlightenment, skewed. I was thought to be what made you happy, you know your good thing. But if I'm a good thing how can this situation be bad. I'm supposed to help you met the vision for us, I never knew the requirement was to have me all covered up. I haven't seen my ankles in ages as if that's a requirement to see my kings face. All the while I've exalted you and you've taken his place.

The church player. Outfit so right it looks like he's graced the covers of a magazine. Gucci loafers, denims starched, with a cardigan to match. And I look plain. Ivory soap washed face with a little shea butter applied. No lip gloss or eye shadow, they don't notice me, a blank canvas at its best. I stand at his side and I notice the eyes.. all.. on.. him. He's claiming to be a church boss but I'm standing here with wrist and ankles covered.. I got this skirt set from Ross!

They're checking me and I'm checking them because my outer appearance doesn't match who I am within, I'm still feisty. Yes, he's my man I warn with my eyes because at some point he forgot. I am confused by you, I see you're enticed by the pencil skirts and the Ruby Woo; but I'm just doing what you suggested, a more natural appearance, you wanted me new! Another one gives me a smile with a message attached that activated something inside of me. I'm trying to figure out are we in this together because it's obvious that you've got a fan club. As we walk passed the heads pop like kernels of corn. Then I figure out, I'm not the only one. I guess they too were intrigued by your knowledge of the word and your charismatic swagger but at this point none of that even matters. I would take off my earrings if I had some on, because my face is already greased. You have deceived me, you've taken the word that is true, wrapped it up in falsehood, and sent me to hell by way of you! Church Player!

I pondered how did I get in this situation and God reminded me what I missed. Getting wrapped up in loneliness because I felt to old to be this single, and everyone else did too. I was to busy trying to make a union that I forgot my first love. All the promises of marriage with no manifestation. We were supposed to be partners, taking the word to the nations. You were going to be my husband I was just doing what you told me to do, you were to be the head of our family and somewhere I forgot that I wasn't even under covenant with you.

I lost it, who I was destined to be. And yes God has a plan even if my skirt stops at my knees.

He's not concerned with the MAC on my face because he's brushed it with grace. I am an asset not an accessory. I don't stand back until you give me the okay to speak, because for some reason you don't think that God speaks through me.

I'm fearfully and wonderfully made, God makes no mistakes. But I do. I was so concerned with being a wife that I began to compromise my ministry for yours. I was misled because you carrying that Bible made me believe that you'd do what's right but I should've known better by your trips to my bedroom by night.

To you sin was bad as long as it wasn't your sin of choice but you made me so I wouldn't have a voice so you wouldn't hear the truth bounce from my lips. So insecure that I won't say this is wrong, keeping quiet in hopes of one day making a home... With you..

How many times have we tried to make the wrong relationship right? How we are clearly defeated but we keep trying to fight. In a voluntary war that God has not cleared, all for the bling, that ring. But at what cost? Eternally attaching ourselves to people that are already married to their egos, slipping on a ring that becomes a noose to your spirit all because you could not wait. Smile sweeps face all because he promised you a ring, now you're late.. The choices that we make.

Church Player! You can find him on a pew near you. Waiting for his next catch, don't let it be you. Sitting around waiting for a husband when there's work to do. So when he comes and stands face to face, look him in the eye and say...I already have a date with a man much greater, so see you later, church player!

XAVIERA L. BELL

In The Furnace: Being Refined Ain't Fun

SEVEN TIMES HOTTER

For several weeks there was a disconnect in our relationship and I couldn't understand why. However, before we ended our usual telephone conversation he surprised me with what he said, "I know that right now it feels strange but trust me it's going to get better. God is doing some things, just be patient. It's going to work out." I couldn't really wrap my head around what he was saying but I believed it to be true. I was due to arrive in Tampa in the next few days and I knew that this was a something that we would discuss when I got there.

I was scheduled to leave by bus, however, God saw fit for me to miss my bus and have to reschedule the trip all together. I left two days later and extended my trip by several days. When arriving in Tampa I was scheduled to meet with my client and settle some things but I later expected to meet with him. It was so crazy that I didn't hear from him, his phone was disconnected and I had no way to reach him. After several days I went to his sister's house to stay for the remainder of my time in the city. For the first time I was able to meet his "spiritual mother" face to face. The woman who was not fond of my existence and that clearly wanted nothing to do with me based on what she had heard from others and not by direct contact.

I recall standing at his sister's kitchen counter

peeling apples for the turnover that I planned to make for dinner. She asked if she could talk to be for a moment. I agreed and we took a seat at the table. Surrounded by his family she served me with news that I was not prepared for. She said, "I hate to be the bearer of bad news but my name is already mud. I told him if he didn't tell you that I would. He's been married for a year. He got married in Jacksonville and he and his wife lives here. No one knew it, not even them." I have never been in a situation where pain, grief, and rage met at the same place. I cried. I wept. I pulled up public record just to confirm. There in my face was the truth. He was married on June 24, 2013 to a woman on the other side of town. I sat in silence and in tears. His spiritual mother says, "See. He decided to marry a real Christian. All the rest of y'all just slept with him. She made him marry her before she jumped in the bed with him. I mean I don't respect any of you because what you want with a man that don't have nothing. When a man is avoiding you, you can't make him be with you. When was the last time you even talked to him?" With a tear streaked face I replied, "This morning when he called to tell me that he was coming to see me today." To say she was shocked is an understatement.

His family apologized and hugged me and surrounded me in love like I was related by blood. His sister who had become a really good friend placed her hand on mine and said while in tears, "I am so sorry. You don't deserve this. You deserve so much better." We cried together. That night I cried myself to sleep. I asked God questions because I needed answers.

The next day he and his wife were no shows to the meeting that we were supposed to have. However, I had advised them previously that he would not show up to face me. Although I didn't know him anymore, somehow I knew him. Accountability was definitely not his area of strength.

I can still feel the pain that I felt as I sat around the dinner table and participated in a prayer that his "spiritual mother" led. I sat there while she prayed for his God ordained marriage, how the devil in hell wouldn't be able to destroy it. As she poured her heart out in prayer I recognized that even in ministry she didn't have a heart for everyone, specifically me. I never experienced people face to face involved in ministry that were pleased at another's brokenness. Although her story was similar to mine, deceived by a married man, she had no empathy for me.

Later that night I was pleasantly surprised to see a little girl who had won my heart when she was 2. When she saw me she said, "Hey Mom! I want to sleep with you tonight." How could I say no? Throughout dinner she referred to me as mom and I knew that everyone at the table did not agree. I knew that this would be a conversation that would be held later. But I didn't care because that's who I had been to her for years. As she lay next to me on the twin sized air mattress she said, "Mom, can me, you, and daddy go to the park?" I said, "Well, daddy and mom aren't friends anymore because daddy has a wife." She looked confused and replied, "So, you and daddy aren't friends anymore because he has a new woman?" In amazement I responded, "Yes." She shook her head and said, "I'm going to talk to daddy tomorrow and let him know that he married the wrong woman. I'm going to tell him.. Daddy, you married the wrong woman, so just marry mom and then we can go to the park and be happy again." As I held her I cried.

The decisions that we make interfere with the lives of others. He didn't think about that when he chose to leave our house, go to the Duval County Courthouse, marry a woman, and come back home to me the same day. We lived in our house for 30 days after he was married, our routine didn't change. We still had dinners together, he still rubbed my feet, he still kissed me, we still had sex every chance that we got. These things ran through my mind on that air mattress. He deceived me and he had cowardly vanished into his existence without even an explanation as to why.

The next morning the daughter to my heart followed me around giving me hugs and kisses. We ate pancakes together and we laughed at any and everything. As I finished my shower I heard her little fist knock on the door. She came into the bathroom and said with tears in her eyes, "Mom, I don't want to go to my daddy's house. I want you to stay here with me." I cried and she cried. I told her, "Mom loves you very much. There are some people that will tell you not to call me mom anymore and I want you to know that this is your choice." She said, "My mom is crying." We hugged and I assured her that I was going to be just fine. The time had come for me to leave and head back home to Alabama. As I gathered my bags I heard her tiny footsteps behind me. Her aunt told her that she couldn't go with us that she would have to stay at the apartment until she returned. With a tremble in her voice she said, "I know. I just want to watch her leave."

I boarded the bus for Orlando and so many thoughts ran through my head. Upon arriving in Orlando I made my way to the smoothie café near my stop. I sat there just tried to gather myself. This was something that was supposed to be happening on a television show, not in my life.

While awaiting the next bus that would take me to Alabama I received a text message. When I opened it I was shocked to find that it was from him. It read, "I'm sorry. I didn't want it to happen this way." Rage filled my being. I was sending text messages so rapidly that he called me. Immediately I answered the phone and said, "How dare you! A year.. You've been married a year. You let me come here be surrounded by your family. You allowed me to be delivered into the hands of a woman that hates me to get satisfaction from delivering me a blow like that. You didn't give me the option of whether or not I wanted to be your whore. Why? All of this? You just told me that you wanted me to wait for you. I'm talking to you about marriage and you have been married for a year. You have a wife. Why? You're begging for time. Were you planning on getting a divorce?" His response was shocking, "Yes. I asked you to marry me and you rejected me. You told me all the things that I needed to do and I was thinking if I save up money for a ring I still have to do other things. To marry her was so easy, all I had to do was take her to the courthouse. As soon as I did it I knew that I had made a big mistake."

When I boarded that bus I cried through several counties. I can remember the glass being so cold on my forehead but the tears were so warm rolling down my cheeks. In a matter of moments my life had changed but all that I could do is continuously play out this scenario in my head.

By the time I made it to Alabama I had no more

tears. I was still grieving because it felt like a death. I contacted him via text and let him know that I need some answers. He called me and we had a conversation. I cried while I was trying to understand the words that escaped his lips but I couldn't. "What do you want me to do? You've had a year to get used to this but I've only learned about this a few days ago. You changed my life without permission. Do you want this marriage? Do you want ministry?" He replied, "I want ministry."

We had a few conversations via text. Him attempting to manipulate me. Calling me telling me that he missed me. Texting me telling me that she had left. Advising me that he wasn't in love and that he was buying his time so that he could just get out. One day I told him to stop texting me that the next time we talked it would be face to face.

The pain that I felt during this time I would never wish on any other woman. I cried, I yelled, I was mad. How scary is it that a man that professes that he loves the Lord can walk out one day, get married to another woman, and come home like nothing had happened. For 12 months, 2 weeks, and 6 days pretended that he wasn't married. For 12 months, 2 weeks, and 6 days hid his wife from your family. For 12 months, 2 weeks, and 6 days he was an adulterer all while working in the church, all while teaching in the church. All while pretending to be a husband that loved and cared for his wife. All while pretending to be a man that loved his girlfriend/fiancé and preparing a future life and ministry.

A man protects and provides for what he loves. He didn't protect me. He wasn't providing for me. He couldn't love me.

It is so essential to the future of women that we don't compromise or sacrifice for men that are not worth it. It doesn't matter how good you are to a person, no matter how much you love them, if they are not loyal, they are just not loyal and you cannot force that. The softer part of us wants to mend and fix them but we never take into consideration that they are probably broken because they destroyed so many women.

I was so tired of hearing that I deserved better, that he was blocking my ministry, hearing that God had to reveal all of this to me so devastatingly so that I would be done for good. But what about my heart. What was I to do about the damage that he had done to my heart? No words were going to fix the damage. I just had to live through this. I had to pray through this. I had to believe through this.

XAVIERA L. BELL

The Transformation: The Day I Got My New Heart

SEVEN TIMES HOTTER

Have you ever hurt so badly that you thought that your heart would just cease to beat? Your very next breath was labored because you were so grieved and you just wanted the pain to stop, immediately. My mind replayed the events of that moment hundreds of times. I thought back to any clues or indications. What did I miss? Was I that desperate? Was I that lost?

I laid in despair because I couldn't imagine how I was going to walk throughout the journey of my life with someone other than the man that I was desperately in love with. He was supposed to be my partner. He was supposed to love me. He was supposed to be the father of my surviving children. However, he abandoned me and our dream of building a ministry for something that I couldn't comprehend, see, or cared to visualize. I couldn't eat for two days. I wept at night so that no one would see me in my weakness.

I cried out to God in the darkness of night while everyone else was asleep. Visions of him sleeping next to another female silhouette haunted my thoughts. "God please help me through this," I begged. I knew that this was a journey that I could not walk alone.

After receiving the care that only a mother can give to a broken hearted daughter, I woke up the morning after returning home and decided that I was going on a walk. With every step joy filled my heart. I started to walk around the community and as I walked God said to me, "It passed over you!" The words were like a lightning bolt through my soul. Then I got it! I put my hands in the air and rejoiced because it could've been me! I could've been caught in a situation with a person that wasn't equipped at the time. I could've been the sacrifice but God said absolutely not, you have a ministry that's in jeopardy. I said, "But I'm feeling different God. Something has changed." He said, "It's okay to have an expiration date on your grieving!"

I was so confused, suddenly I felt different. Don't get me wrong, I was still hurting but I was anticipating the other side of hurt.. healing.

Some of us are still crying over a situation that God saved us from! God says write a date of expiration and on that day your grieving will be over! Count it all joy that it passed over you! You weren't in the plans of demise! It passed over you so that it could position you! Your pain is for a purpose! Your pain is perfecting you! God had to make it better and he didn't want it to be at your expense. Oh the BLOOD!

Seven Times Hotter: The Day the Heat Was Turned Up

SEVEN TIMES HOTTER

XAVIERA L. BELL

In October 2014 I received a job offer in Tampa, Florida and I relocated. I think that inside I thought that God was bringing our paths back together and to me it didn't matter that he had a wife. When I looked him in his face and although it illuminated betrayal I loved him still. I made up in my mind that I didn't care what anyone said, no he didn't deserve me but I wanted what I wanted and I didn't care what it cost.

Although we weren't together we were together. We went on dates and went to concerts. I was even his emergency contact. The irony of his job calling me and not his wife when he was ill. I can recall one night sitting at the hospital with him holding his cell phone and his wife called. As I looked at her picture with her name it occurred to me that she was not a stranger at all. This woman was his so called prayer partner. Thoughts ran through my head and I saw red. The fact that we were in the hospital probably saved his life and prevented me from a long run at the state pen. She knew me! Wow! I started to wonder what happened to the female culture. When was it ever okay to have a relationship with another woman's husband and not even care, when was it okay to marry a man that lived with his fiancé and allow him to return to their home for a month while you lived on the other side of town.

The turbulence of it all was sickening. Him getting caught and her being broken but not strong enough to leave. Him coming to my home with 2 dozen roses, cards, gifts, and me not caring that he would return home, to his wife. The one that he was legally bound to. The one that he shared a home and a bed with just like we used to. In my head she was a diluted version of me.

In November 2014 I grew very ill. I had been staying at his family's home sleeping on an air mattress in the corner trying to re-establish my life after a lay off. I went to the doctor and they really couldn't find anything wrong. In ten days I lost 11lbs. I received a call from someone advising me that it wasn't a physical illness. My mother spoke to me and she said that she had a dream that someone was feeding me something to make me sick. I asked the Lord to reveal what was happening and he gave me a dream. I thought that I was being bitter so I asked for confirmation. In January 2015, my church was having a revival. The guest pastor asked everyone to come up front so that he could touch and agree with them for the year. I made my way to the front and he looked at me and said, "What they sent to you was meant to kill you! But the spirit of the Lord protected you from harm." I knew what he meant.

Even after that confirmation I continued to see him. In May I began sharing a house with a couple and in September I moved into my own apartment and he continued to come on a more regular basis. He made it his business to come over and rub my feet and take showers and cook meals. The closer we became the more I was convinced that the divorce papers that were on my computer would be filed. I guess the joke was on me as it usually was.

November 2015 I received the most heart wrenching news that I could have ever imagined. A man that was a father figure passed away. The day that he passed away was the day that my ex fiancé decided that we weren't going to speak any more. I was more upset than hurt because on all the days in the calendar year, he chose the most painful. I knew that this was it for us and I was okay with the conclusion of this horrendous story. During this time I could only think back to the man that I affectionately called "Jay" and how he loved me from the day that I took my first breath. That there was nothing that he wouldn't do for me. He loved me and when I measured his love against the man that I thought was going to be my husband, Jay's far exceeded his.

A month and a half after Jay's death I received an inbox on Facebook from my childhood minister. She advised that she had a dream about my ex pursuing me. I advised her that I had not spoken to him in nearly two months. She told me to prepare because he was coming back. Three days later he showed up at my house in the middle of a panic attack because he said that he just had to see me.

I recognized that the magnetic attraction was not going to cease unless one of us did a 180. Well into the next year we saw each other. He was a frequent visitor, however, the interaction changed. I was no longer in love. I loved him but I was no longer in love with him and his presence was no longer a requirement. I didn't need to see him and I didn't need to share my bed with him.

I figured out something very important about him. He loved his wife for the very thing he despised me for, she needed him and I didn't. In that moment I learned that my ego kept me attached to him. My ego was bruised and all this time I thought that my heart was guiding my emotions, it was my pride. For so many of us women we pick apart the new woman, she's not as cute.. She doesn't have a degree.. But she has the man that once was mine. I grieved for the woman that I used to be. I was an advocate for women and here I am tearing this woman's house apart and her husband was a willing participant.

I grew tired of hearing that I was better than him. I was tired of hearing that he was not equipped for where God was taking me. I was tired of hearing that he was a downgrade. Because for three years he was who I was preparing to marry. This situation damaged a great part of my heart but it also damaged the people that were cheering us on as a couple. Many believed that it was a phase and others believed that it was divine intervention, the very hand of God separated us so that we could individually work in our respective capacities. Because of spite I was holding on to a relationship that had expired thinking that one day he would just leave, then I realized that no matter what you say audibly, your actions speak volumes. He loved walking out of the house and getting into her car and making late night visits, he loved going to see Jill Scott and Floetry with me and having intellectual conversations about his dreams, God, and business. I watched him look at the phone screen and dismiss her calls and my heart shifted. I could never ever trust him based on his actions and impulsive decision making.

The last conversation that we had he was bothered because he wanted me to get pregnant and I wouldn't. I guess the Scarlet Letter wasn't bright enough. He wanted me to get pregnant so that she would leave him because honestly he just didn't have the courage to leave her. He didn't want to be the bad guy twice.

As the flames of this situation burned the core of

me I recognized that never should one be in a situation with a person and they decide to be with them by default. The strategic plan behind the pregnancy was so that my character and effectiveness would be tarnished and diminished. We forget as women that we are birthers, however, we get linked up with people that rape us of the opportunity to produce, and we become barren.

If I didn't live this life I would be certain that this was a fictitious movie that came on LMN on Sunday night. Unfortunately it is not. Ever tear I shed I remember. Every scream that escaped my mouth I recall. The deep planted seed of rejection I felt take root inside. All the advice I gave women I didn't heed to myself. What can I advise you as a reader? It's so simplistic. You my friend are the author that pens your great ending. When are you going to change your characters? Don't die in a furnace that was built for someone else. There's so much more to live for. You deserve the best.

BUT.. Me telling you and you believing is a totally different thing. No matter how we want someone to change and how badly we desire them it is left up with them if they make steps to change. There is no convincing a person that you are the better option. If you are ever in a situation where you have to convince someone that you are great, you are in the wrong situation. You are wonderful!

You don't have to be in compromising situations with unfavorable circumstances to persuade an individual that is undeserving of you. Would I change my story? No. I recognize that the hell that I went through was so that I could write this book for you. The tears that saturated the pillows on countless nights was so that you could read this book. The yoyo love story was so that you could be convinced that if he chose someone else, he just wasn't for you. Did you do anything wrong, possibly. But you don't deserve to be lied to and lied on. What I know about my ex is that the lies he fed her were just as powerful as the ones that he fed me. Never will I say that this journey was not difficult, it was tremendously painful. However, one day you will wake up and not cry anymore. One day you will go to bed and realize that you didn't think about him today. And one day you will realize that the furnace isn't fun but it is certainly necessary.

My desire for you is to know that you can heal and live a victorious life. You can see him in passing and your smile and salutation will be genuine. Heal, with time. Progress, with time. Know that he will never be able to repay you in this life for the pain and possible damage that was caused. Your progression is wrapped in process. Go through it.. Don't live in it!

SEVEN TIMES HOTTER

XAVIERA L. BELL

My Transparent Moment: The Ashes Weren't Beautiful

SEVEN TIMES HOTTER

I wanted to close this book out with something that was transparent, something that was real, and something that would initiate growth in you right in the place that you are in. So often I have played this story out in my mind. Even the more I have cried and I have battled with the thoughts of "what if".

Let me tell you what I know as an expert in the field of heartbreak and recovery. The ugly truth is that the very act of being hurt and broken has a detrimental effect on your person as a whole. Physically I couldn't eat or I binged, emotionally I was tapped out, and mentally I was on the verge of losing it. But the harshest reality was when I looked in the face of my own demons. My ego was damaged because I had been demoted from a fiancé to a side chick. And the even more ugly part about it is that I didn't care because I wanted to hurt her because she knowingly hurt me.

I had become bitter and the ongoing affair between he and I made tolerating my pain a bit more manageable. I singlehandedly strategized to cause havoc in their household and he was a willing participant, because he too didn't care. What he figured out is that having what you want and what you need simultaneously was way better.

I felt powerful knowing that he craved me and that the longest that he could ever stay away was

45 days. I was energized at the attention a blocked phone number could get and the fact that he would compromise his household, cancel their plans if he heard an ounce of disappointment in my tone.

What had I become? I wanted what I wanted and what I wanted was him. Even though he hurt me, I wanted him. Even though he betrayed me, I wanted him. There was nothing that a person could say to me that could change the craving in my heart for the man that I almost had a family with. Even today I struggle with the hopes of one day him waking up and realizing that he made a mistake. But then again, what would be the cost attached to the heartbreak that I suffered. Would he ever be able to pay that debt in full?

I struggled to write the ugliest part of me because I have never seen it in words.

These next sentences are what you have to intake for your own self-preservation in this critical time if you are battling with heartbreak. It is painful to love someone who loves you but doesn't choose you. It is even the more painful to see them on a consistent basis and recognize that you added so much more to their lives. It is confusing to have a clear ally divide. You have one group in your ear telling you how things will work out and that he had to go find himself so that he can become better for you. Then you have the other group telling you that he will never leave his wife, that you were too good for him, and that you would be a fool to take him back. My all-time favorite is the conflicting prophesies that were spoken on God's behalf, which can leave anyone confused. Then you have him! The one who has your heart and your ear, whispering that he's coming back and that everything will be okay.. That he will work for the rest of his life making it right because you deserve every great and wonderful thing.

This is the most critical and impressionable space in time because all you crave is direction just to find that you are being pulled in so many. The only thing that will save you is silence. Uninterrupted by the opinions of others. Be still and silent. Rest in the pain of the experience. Nurse your wounds and place the salve of the process on your heart. Buy a beautiful shade of lipstick and stand in the mirror and look at the beauty that pain produced. Nothing about your beauty has changed, nothing about your value has diminished, and nothing about your substance has become questionable. You've just become a masterpiece. There is not another like you, so stop comparing, you still measure up! Know that even in this moment... YOU'RE A BIG DEAL!

SEVEN TIMES HOTTER

A LETTER FROM THE AUTHOR

Xaviera L. Bell, M.S.

Exodus_Project@outlook.com

www.exodus-project.com

Hey Beautiful,

I wanted you to know that I wrote this book with you in mind. I weighed my options. I thought what would happen to her if she didn't get the opportunity to see first-hand that hurt just isn't that painful always. I can remember sitting in my own despair. I remember the saltiness of my tears mixed with the bitterness of my own self-appointed defeat. How intoxicating and heavy it was just to carry the burden of being hurt from day to day.

I know personally how painful it is to have an event to transpire that changes the total direction of your life. I know how it feels for a chapter of your life to be closed and you didn't give permission for the scene to end. I know what it is like to wait on something that never arrives and how each day you will your heart to stop because it's so extremely damaged that the very fact that it is beating is miraculous. I also know how it feels to wake up and be able to breathe a little less labored.

Throughout this turbulent time of my life I realized an important fact. I realized that this snapshot in time does not determine who I am, what I am worth, or what I will become after it's over.. And it will be over.

I chose to depart my place of despair and I encourage you to do the same. You deserve it. You are worth it!

Never underestimate your ability to recreate yourself. Every weak place provides you with an area of opportunity. Every break or bruise allows you to mend. Every day of rain gives you the expectation of sunshine.

You are phenomenal and my expectation for you is to be better than you were yesterday, to create a new you for tomorrow, and live the best life you can live on today.

Great things are ahead for you. If you give up now.. You'll never see all the wonderful things that you are destined to reap. Keep going!

www.ingramcontent.com/pod-product-compliance
Lightning Source LLC
Chambersburg PA
CBHW060034050426
42448CB00012B/3005